Ladybugs, Bees & Butterfly Trees

MATILDA NORDTVEDT

BETHANY HOUSE PUBLISHERS
MINNEAPOLIS, MINNESOTA 55438
A Division of Bethany Fellowship, Inc.

Copyright © 1985
Matilda Nordtvedt
All Rights Reserved

Published by Bethany House Publishers
A Division of Bethany Fellowship, Inc.
6820 Auto Club Road, Minneapolis, MN 55438

Printed in the United States of America

Library of Congress Cataloging in Publication Data

Nordtvedt, Matilda
    Ladybugs, bees, and butterfly trees.

    Summary: Poems about a wide variety of animals present lessons in Christian living and are accompanied by Bible verses, study questions, and prayers.
    1. Animals—Religious aspects—Christianity—Juvenile literature. 2. Children—Prayer-books and devotions—English. [1. Animals—Religious aspects—Christianity—Poetry. 2. Christian life—Poetry. 3. American poetry. 4. Prayer books and devotions] I. Title.
BT746.N67 1985   242'.62   84-24343
ISBN 0-87123-820-9

Especially for our grandchildren: Kjerstin,
Micah, Erika, Annalise, Joshua, Brittany and David

MATILDA NORDTVEDT is a pastor's wife and homemaker living in Everett, Wash. She has also spent eight years in Japan as a missionary. Her writing career includes both curriculum materials and many books. This is her second book with Bethany House.

Contents

Ladybugs, Bees & Butterfly Trees

Bears

Baby Bear is oh so small
    the day that he is born.
He doesn't have much hair at all.
    You'd think he had been shorn.

At first he drinks his mother's milk,
    but as he older grows,
he has to learn to search for food;
    this his mother knows.

She need not teach him how to swim
    nor how to climb a tree.
Baby Bear knows how to do
    these things quite naturally.

The important lesson for Baby Bear
    is learning to obey.
When Mother Bear says, "Climb that tree,"
    there is no other way.

Danger is near—maybe a wolf,
    or even a man with a gun.
When Mother Bear says, "Baby, run,"
    Baby Bear had better run!

Bible Verse:

"Children, obey your parents" (Eph. 6:1).

Questions:

1. Why does Mother Bear make her cubs mind?
2. What would happen to the cub if he disobeyed?
3. Why do your parents insist that you obey?

Prayer:

Dear Jesus, please help me to be obedient even when it's hard.

Pecking Chickens

Chickens sometimes are not kind,
　　they peck at one another.
Each one wants to be the boss
　　and shoo away his brother.

The pecked chick gets very thin;
　　his feathers are a sight,
because he's fussed and bothered so
　　by chicks who like to fight.

God says, "Be kind to everyone,"
　　I hope that you have heard.
That awful pecking system—well,
　　it's only "for the birds."

Bible Verse:

"Be kind to one another" (Eph. 4:32).

Questions:

1. Why do some chickens peck other chickens?
2. What happens to the pecked chickens?
3. When you are unkind to your friends, how do they feel?
4. Think of two ways you can be kind to a brother, sister or a friend.

Prayer:

Dear Jesus, please help me to be kind to my family and friends and never hit or pinch.

Animal Cooperation

A rhinoceros is big and fierce,
  we know that for a fact.
But the tiny tickbird's not afraid;
  he rides right on his back.

The rhino likes the little bird
  because he helps him out.
He eats the ticks that bother him,
  that make him snarl and pout.

The tiny bird likes rhino, too—
  on his back he finds his dinner.
Besides, his transportation's free.
  Now isn't that a winner?

If I would like to have a friend,
  first I a friend must be:
helpful, kind, considerate,
  not thinking just of me.

Bible Verse:

"There is a friend who sticks closer than a brother" (Prov. 18:24).

Questions:

1. How does the tickbird help the rhinoceros?
2. How does the rhinoceros help the tickbird?
3. Think of two ways you can help your friend.

Prayer:

Dear Jesus, thank You for being my very best Friend. Help me to be a good friend to others.

Pine Caterpillars

Pine caterpillars are followers—
    it really is a shame.
They look to see what others do,
    and then they do the same.

They follow the one ahead of them,
    round and round they go.
Where is their destination?
    Sadly, they do not know.

There's only one to follow,
    that's Jesus—oh, how true!
He'll guide you safely through this life,
    lead you to Heaven, too!

Bible Verse:

"Jesus said, 'Follow me' " (Matt. 4:19).

Questions:

1. Why does the pine caterpillar always follow the leader?
2. Why do children want to do what others do?
3. Why is it sometimes good to be different?
4. Whom should we follow?

Prayer:

Dear Jesus, I will follow and obey You no matter what my playmates do.

Kangaroo

How can you weigh two hundred pounds
   when you are only two?
I know you were an inch at birth.
   Whatever did you do?

"Within my mother's pouch I drank
   nutritious milk—you bet!
Soon I was eating grasses, too,
   and I am growing yet.

"Would you like to grow big and strong
   like me, Joe Kangaroo?
Drink your milk and eat your food,
   all that is given you."

Bible Verse:

"Eat what is set before you" (Luke 10:8).

Questions:

1. How big was Joey Kangaroo when he was born?
2. How big was he when he turned two years old?
3. How did he get so big?
4. How can you grow big and strong?

Prayer:

Thank You, God, for all the good food You give to us.

Animal Disguises

The bittern is a clever bird;
    her Creator made her so,
she sways right with the cattails
    when the gentle breezes blow.

The dead leaf butterfly looks so bright
    as long as she is flying,
but when she lights upon a branch,
    she looks like a leaf that's dying.

The crab he wears a sponge on his shell.
    Sshh—it's surely a disguise.
He's hiding from his enemies.
    How can he be so wise?

Bible Verse:

"Who is a teacher like Him?" (Job 36:22).

Questions:

1. How does the bittern hide from her enemies?
2. How does the dead leaf butterfly hide?
3. What does the crab wear on his shell to hide under?
4. How do these creatures know how to keep safe?

Prayer:

Dear Jesus, You teach the animals and birds how to keep safe. Thank You for teaching me, too—especially from the Bible.

Oysters

The oyster opens his shell real wide
    to let the warm sea in.
His gills pick out the food he needs;
    the water flows out again.

But what is this? A grain of sand?
    Ouch, it hurts! He squirms.
He makes some shell to cover it,
    and makes some more again.

The years go by, and then one day,
    the oyster's in a whirl.
The pesky sand he didn't like
    has turned into a pearl!

Bible Verse:

"God causes all things to work together for good to those who love God" (Rom. 8:28).

Questions:

1. Where does the oyster get his food?
2. Why doesn't he like the grain of sand?
3. What does he do with it? What does it turn into?
4. Is there something you don't like?
5. What does God say about it?

Prayer:

Dear Jesus, help me not to cry when Daddy leaves on a trip or when I fall off my tricycle. I learn and grow through hard things.

Monarch Butterfly

The monarch butterfly starts his life
    on a milkweed plant so green.
He eats and eats the milky juice
    that flows through the leaf's veins.

The milkweed tastes so bitter;
    other animals and bugs say, "Yuk."
Monarch butterfly thinks that's great;
    it means that he's in luck.

For if he eats the bitter leaves
    of the milkweed plant all day,
his enemies won't touch him;
    he'll taste the very same way!

Bible Verse:

"Who is like the Lord our God?" (Ps. 113:5).

Questions:

1. What does the monarch butterfly eat?
2. How does this help him?
3. Who figured all this out for him?

Prayer:

Dear Jesus, You think of everything, even a way to protect the monarch butterflies from being eaten. Thank You for planning for me, too.

Brown Thrasher

Little brown thrasher, why do you sing
    so high up in the tree?
"I'm calling for a mate to come
    and make a nest with me."

Little brown bird, you have a mate;
    now just why do you sing?
"To keep the other birds away
    from where I am the king."

Little brown bird, how did you learn
    to sing up in the tree?
"God gave me parents to teach me how,
    tweedle-deedle, dee."

Bible Verse:

"Sing to the Lord, all the earth" (Ps. 96:1).

Questions:

1. Why does the little lonesome bird sing in the tree?
2. Why does he sing after he has a mate?
3. Why do you sing?
4. What does God think of our songs to Him?

Prayer:

Dear Jesus, I will sing a song to You every day and praise You.

Killdeer

The killdeer puts on a clever act
    to protect her young from harm.
She pretends to be lame and flap her wings
    as she cries out in alarm.

Her enemy follows her, thinking he
    will find where her babies lie.
But just before he reaches her,
    she soars into the sky.

We, too, have an enemy;
    it's Satan, oh, he's clever.
But Jesus helps us run from him.
    Don't do what he says—ever!

Bible Verse:

"Resist the devil" (James 4:7).

Questions:

1. How does the killdeer protect her young?
2. Who is our enemy? What does he want us to do?
3. Who helps us say no to him?

Prayer:

Dear Jesus, help me to say no when Satan tempts me to be disobedient to my parents.

Polar Bear

Polar bear, why are you white
    instead of black or brown?
"So I'll blend right in with the snow
    when enemies come round."

Polar bear, why do you wear
    a heavy coat of fur?
"My Creator gave me this fine coat
    so I'd keep warm for sure."

How can you see to find your food
    when the sun glares on the ice?
"I have sunglasses you can't see,
    they're built right in my eyes."

Bible Verse:

"O Lord, how many are Thy works! In wisdom Thou hast made them all" (Ps. 104:24).

Questions:

1. Why is the polar bear white?
2. Why does he have a heavy coat?
3. Why does he need sunglasses in his eyes?
4. Who made the wonderful polar bear?

Prayer:

Dear Jesus, You take such good care of polar bears. Thank You for taking care of me, too.

Dolphin

The dolphin's playful and very smart;
    he can learn many things.
He waves his flippers to make folks laugh
    and jumps through hoops and rings.

He pushes fish into men's nets,
    he swims many, many a mile;
but best of all, he always greets
    the folks he meets with a smile.

Now you are just a little girl,
    or maybe you're a boy.
But if you smile instead of pout,
    you'll bring folks lots of joy.

Bible Verse:

"Be glad in the Lord" (Ps. 32:11).

Questions:

1. What are some tricks dolphins can learn?
2. How do dolphins greet people?
3. Name three people you can smile at today.

Prayer:

Dear Jesus, help me to give away lots of smiles today and make others happy.

Chameleon

A chameleon can change his shade
    from brown or gray to green.
It is a very clever way
    to hide and not be seen.

He changes his color to match his mood—
    that's one of his tricks, too.
When he is feeling grumpy,
    he'll turn gray for you.

Now you can't change your color
    like the chameleon so clever.
But you can wear a great big smile,
    frown never, never, never!

Bible Verse:

"Rejoice always" (1 Thess. 5:16).

Questions:

1. Why does the chameleon change his color?
2. What does it mean when a chameleon turns gray?
3. How can we get rid of frowns?

Prayer:

Dear Jesus, when I pout and frown I make folks sad. Help me to turn my frowns upside down so they'll be smiles.

Ants

Cowboy ants tend aphid
    which give off honeydew drops.
Baby ants like aphid "milk"
    better than lollipops.

In wintertime ant cowboys
    hide their "cows" in tunnel barns.
In summer they'll get more milk from them
    so must keep them safe from harm.

The ant cowboys work so hard.
    "Be like them," God tells us.
When Mom and Daddy ask for help,
    pitch in without a fuss.

Bible Verse:

"Go to the ant . . . observe her ways and be wise" (Prov. 6:6).

Questions:

1. What insects are the ants' "cows"?
2. What kind of "milk" do they give?
3. Why do the ant cowboys put them in underground barns?
4. Name two things you can do to help at home.

Prayer:

Dear Jesus, help me to learn from the hard-working ants to help at home and not be lazy.

Fleas

Although a flea's a tiny bug,
   much damage he can do.
He bites your legs and makes them itch;
   your dog he bothers, too.

Whole armies have been defeated
   by pesty insects such as these.
Fleas have changed the course of hist'ry
   by spreading dread disease.

Fleas make us think of little sins:
   a sneaky act, a lie.
If we let them stay within our hearts,
   they'll ruin us by and by.

Bible Verse:

"Create in me a clean heart, O God" (Ps. 51:10).

Questions:

1. What happens to your leg when a flea bites it?
2. What do fleas often spread?
3. Why are fleas like little sins?

Prayer:

Dear Jesus, forgive me for the little sins I often forget about.

Migration

Birds fly south for the winter.
  It's really an excellent plan.
It's not to visit relatives
  nor to get a good suntan.

Birds have a definite reason—
  lack of food makes them go.
Insects are gone in north's wintertime;
  seeds lie buried in snow.

Back they fly to their home in the north
  as soon as it becomes spring.
There's no place like home, no place at all!
  They build their nests and sing.

The days grow longer, there's food again;
    it's time for a new family.
Mother bird lays her eggs in the nest;
    Father bird sings in the tree.

The birds are thankful for food and home,
    though they don't know it comes from above.
But we know and are thankful to our God
    for all His blessings and love.

Bible Verse:

"Every good thing bestowed and every perfect gift is from above" (James 1:17).

Questions:

1. Why do birds fly south in the wintertime?
2. What do they do in the spring?
3. What are some things we should be thankful for?

Prayer:

Dear Jesus, thank You for food to eat and a home to live in.

Lemmings

Far away in northern climes
    live lemmings underground.
There they have their families
    where food and space abound.

But as the baby lemmings grow,
    they have families of their own.
The tunnels get so crowded,
    they no longer feel like home.

Some decide to leave their house;
    they march right into the sea.
They don't know how wide it is
    and drown. What a pity!

Our world is getting crowded, too,
   but we don't need to fuss.
Jesus is fixing a beautiful home
   up in Heaven for us.

Bible Verse:

"I go to prepare a place for you" (John 14:2).

Questions:

1. Where do lemmings live?
2. Why do they have to leave their home?
3. Where do they go?
4. What is Jesus preparing for us?

Prayer:

Dear Jesus, thank You for preparing a place in Heaven for me.

Glowworm and Snail

Though glowworm's smaller than the snail,
    he'd like the snail for dinner.
How can he conquer such a prize?
    How can he be the winner?

The snail has shells, too hard to bite;
    if he rests on a rock,
no enemy can hurt him;
    it's like a house that's locked.

But sometimes the snail gets careless;
    he rests on a grassy stem—
two folds of flesh peep out his shell;
    the glowworm soon is there.

He taps the flesh with his hooked fangs.
 He eats the snail for dinner.
If snail had only stayed on a rock,
 he would have been the winner.

You our enemy is Satan.
 When he comes to tempt and mock,
be sure you run to Jesus.
 Jesus is your Rock.

Bible Verse:

"Who is like a rock, besides our God?" (2 Sam. 22:32).

Questions:

1. What mistake did the snail make?
2. Who is our Rock?
3. How can He help us against our enemy?

Prayer:

Dear Jesus, thank You for being my Rock where I can be safe.

Turtle

Mom Turtle does not sit on her eggs
    which she has laid in the earth.
She's too cold; she must wait for the sun
    to warm and bring them to birth.

One day they hatch. Oh, aren't they cute!
    So tiny, and each has a shell.
It's soft at first, but will harden soon
    and protect them very well.

The shell is where the turtle lives,
    wherever he goes, it goes too.
He never has to rent a room,
    his turtle shell will do.

The shell's his armor, too, you see;
　　it really is a dandy.
When danger's near he ducks inside.
　　Now isn't that quite handy?

God gives us protection, too—
　　from Satan, the world, and sin.
When we are tempted to do wrong,
　　we can run right to Him!

Bible Verse:

"God is a refuge for us" (Ps. 62:8).

Questions:

1. Why doesn't Mother Turtle sit on her eggs?
2. What is the turtle's protection?
3. Who is our protection?

Prayer:

Dear Jesus, thank You that I can run to You when I am afraid or tempted to do wrong.

Owl

The owl is clever at finding food.
    Little mouse and squirrel beware!
His ears are sensitive and so big,
    he always knows you're there.

He glides noiselessly through the air;
    his wings don't make a sound.
It's very easy for him to swoop
    an animal up from the ground.

He's good at frightening creatures, too;
    puffs up his feathers to look scary.
It makes his enemies run away
    and everyone be wary.

When he is looking for a mate,
the owl lady is not sure
if he has come to court and woo
or make big trouble for her.

Who made the owl so smart, so wise,
so he knows what to do?
God gave him wisdom just as He
will give you wisdom, too.

Bible Verse:

"Give me understanding" (Ps. 119:34).

Questions:

1. What helps the owl to find food to eat?
2. Who made the owl wise?
3. How can you be wise?

Prayer:

Dear Jesus, help me to understand Your words and be wise.

Penguin

Penguins have no nests at all.
    That doesn't seem so nice.
Mama lays her precious egg
    right on the freezing ice!

Papa Penguin comes to help—
    he'll keep the new egg warm.
He rolls it in a fold of skin
    and keeps it from all harm.

Meanwhile, Mama Penguin takes a trip—
    for two whole months she feeds.
Not only for herself she eats,
    but for her baby's needs.

She comes back from the open sea;
>   her baby hatches soon.
She feeds him from her own stomach;
>   her beak serves for a spoon.

The penguins are good parents;
>   I'm sure you agree.
God has given us parents, too.
>   How thankful we should be!

Bible Verse:

"His mother would make him a little robe" (1 Sam. 2:19).

Questions:

1. How does Papa Penquin keep the egg warm?
2. How does Mama Penguin get food to feed her baby?
3. What do your parents do for you?

Prayer:

Dear Jesus, thank You for giving me parents to care for me.

Beaver

Beavers grow up very fast.
   When they are only two,
their father guides them up the stream,
   says, "Build a house for you."

The beaver knows just what to do;
   in his house three rooms he'll make—
two small, one large and entries two,
   underwater, for escape.

Since Beaver *swims* into his home,
   he always comes in wet.
The small rooms are for drying off,
   the large room's where he sits.

The beaver makes a storeroom, too,
   complete with food supply.
The pond will soon freeze over,
   and he must eat or die.

Little beaver, you are wise,
   for winter to prepare.
I, too, must ready be to meet
   my Savior in the air.

Bible Verse:

"Prepare to meet your God" (Amos 4:12).

Questions:

1. How many rooms does the beaver's house have?
2. What does he eat when the pond freezes?
3. How can you prepare to meet God?

Prayer:

Thank You, Jesus, for forgiving my sins so I can go up to Heaven with You when You come back.

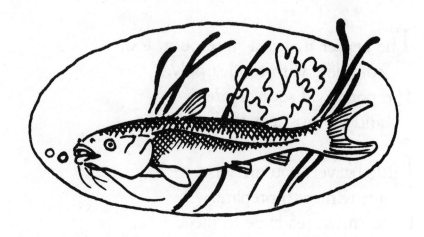

Sea Catfish

The sea can be a scary place,
    for enemies lurk near.
The sea catfish know what to do.
    Their offspring need not fear.

Mom sea catfish lays her eggs,
    Dad hides them, oh, so quick.
He keeps them safe right in his mouth.
    Now that is quite a trick.

Poor Daddy cannot eat a thing—
    his mouth must stay closed tight.
He loves his babies very much.
    He says, "Oh, that's all right."

For weeks he keeps his mouth shut tight
   until those small eggs hatch.
Dad catfish breathes a grateful sigh;
   he can open his mouth at last!

Bible Verse:

"A father has compassion on his children" (Ps. 103:13).

Questions:

1. What does the sea catfish father do for his children?
2. What does your father do for you?
3. Do you thank your father for providing for you?

Prayer:

Dear Jesus, thank You for my daddy.

Nose

Everybody has a nose—
  people and animals, too.
It doesn't seem much use at all,
  but it has a job to do.

Many animals find their food
  by smelling out their prey.
Sharks can smell their victims
  from a quarter mile away.

A swordfish's nose is five feet long;
  he uses it like a sword.
A seahorse has a tubelike snout
  to siphon out his food.

You would look very strange indeed
    if you had no nose.
How could you smell danger, such as fire,
    or the lovely smell of a rose?

God made everything for a reason;
    He is so very wise.
Thank Him for giving you a nose
    as well as mouth and eyes.

Bible Verse:

"Oh, the depth of the riches both of the wisdom and knowledge of God!" (Rom. 11:33).

Questions:

1. What are noses for?
2. Why is this important for animals? For you?
3. Who gave you your nose?

Prayer:

Thank You, Jesus, for giving me a nose to smell with.

Eagles

Papa and Mama Eagle mate for life.
　　They take turns sitting on their eggs.
Their scraggly little eaglets
　　have gray down and skinny legs.

They quickly grow and soon begin
　　to exercise in the nest.
It's so they can jump about
　　and give their wings a stretch.

One day when they are thirteen weeks
　　the time has come to try
their wings out on a real flight
　　way up there in the sky.

At first they are so afraid
　　(I'm sure they feel like crying).
But as they start and stretch their wings,
　　they find that they are flying.

We shouldn't be afraid to try
　　even something that's hard to do.
The Lord who helps the eaglet
　　will surely help us, too!

Bible Verse:

"The Lord is my helper" (Heb. 13:6).

Questions:

1. How do the eaglets learn to fly?
2. What hard thing does the Lord want you to do?
3. Who will help you?

Prayer:

Dear Jesus, thank You for being my helper. Help me to try like the eaglets.

Bird Nests

The tailorbird knows how to sew;
    her thread is fiber or grass.
She laces it through leaves so broad
    to make herself a nest.

Why is that hornbill imprisoned with mud
    into her hole in the tree?
Her mate did that to keep their eggs safe;
    only her beak is free.

When Mrs. Hummingbird builds her nest,
    there are certain things that she knows.
If she uses plant down and cobwebs,
    it will stretch as her family grows.

God has made the birds of the air
   very wise, don't you agree?
Surely He has a wonderful plan
   also for you and me!

Bible Verse:

"The Mighty One has done great things for me" (Luke 1:49).

Questions:

1. How does the tailorbird make her nest?
2. Why does the male hornbill plaster his wife into the nest?
3. Who taught the hummingbird how to make a nest?

Prayer:

Thank You, God, for what You teach me.

Feathers

Birds have amazing clothes to wear,
    undies and raincoat in one.
Their feathers keep them warm and dry,
    the quill, the barbs, the down.

The down is soft like your p.j.'s;
    they wear it next to their skin.
Their feathers are oiled to shed the rain
    and keep their body heat in.

God takes care of the birds of the air;
    He forgets not even one.
How much more will He care for you
    who are His daughter or son!

Bible Verse:

"He cares for you" (1 Pet. 5:7).

Questions:

1. What kind of underclothes do birds wear?
2. What kind of raincoat did God give to birds?
3. How does God care for you?

Prayer:

Thank You, God, for taking care of the birds and me, too.

Termites

What does a termite like to eat—
     cereal or other food?
Oh no, this creature of the dirt
     chooses to feed on wood!

These insects live far underground;
     they hide by night and day.
A bird or spider, lizards, too,
     might eat them if they stray.

They tunnel right up from the ground
     and find some rotting wood:
a stump or log, they do not care—
     to them it all tastes good.

Sometimes they eat new lumber, too,
   a post, a door, a wall.
When they have chewed the inside out,
   the strongest wood will fall.

Termites are just like little sins—
   a thought, a deed, a lie.
If they are in your life house now,
   tell them at once, "Good-bye!"

Bible Verse:

"Be sure your sin will find you out" (Num. 32:23).

Questions:

1. What does a termite eat?
2. What happens to a post when a termite attacks it?
3. What happens when we let little sins stay in our lives?

Prayer:

Dear Jesus, please forgive me for _____ and _____.
Thank You for forgiving me.

Pigeon

The pigeon mother lays an egg
    or even may lay two.
Her mate, the cock, helps keep them warm;
    he is a daddy true.

When the eggs hatch, oh me, oh my,
    the squabs are blind and bare.
But give them time, soon they will see
    and feathers will appear.

The baby pigeons grow four weeks;
    their training then will start.
They learn to find their way right home.
    Now, don't you think they're smart?

Pigeons are useful as can be—
    no matter where they roam.
If you tie a message on their leg,
    they will bring it home.

Bible Verse:

"Let the redeemed of the Lord say so" (Ps. 107:2).

Questions:

1. What does the newborn pigeon look like?
2. What do pigeons learn to do that is different from other birds?
3. What message can you bring your friends?

Prayer:

Dear Jesus, help me to tell my friends that I love You.

Butterfly Trees

Pretty butterfly is flying south;
    winter has come, you see.
He must go back to the old homeplace;
    he must fly to the butterfly tree.

He has never, never been there before.
    How can he know the way?
God gave him a compass to guide him there,
    and a clock to tell how long to stay.

God has given you a compass, too,
    your conscience, a tiny voice
that tells you what's right and what is wrong,
    and then you make your choice.

Bible Verse:

"We will obey His voice" (Josh. 24:24).

Questions:

1. How can the butterfly find the butterfly tree?
2. How does he know how long to stay?
3. Do you sometimes hear a tiny voice telling you not to do something?
4. What did God give us for our compass?

Prayer:

Dear Jesus, help me to listen to the tiny voice in my heart that tells me to stop when I'm about to do something naughty.

Ladybug

Nobody swats at ladybugs
    or kills them with a spray.
They are our friends; they help us out.
    We won't send them away.

The ladybug is popular,
    does not annoy or sting.
She helps the farmers with their crops,
    eats every pesty thing.

If you do not annoy or tease,
    are helpful, kind and true,
you'll be like the ladybug,
    folks will like you, too!

Bible Verse:

"And just as you want men to treat you, treat them in the same way" (Luke 6:31).

Questions:

1. Why do people swat some insects?
2. Why do they like ladybugs?
3. How can you help people to like you?

Prayer:

Dear Jesus, help me to be helpful like the ladybug and to not tease and annoy those around me.

Bowerbird

"I like blue," says the bowerbird,
    "In Australia is my nest.
I drag home anything I can find
    that's blue—I like it best.

"If you look carefully in my nest,
    you'll see lots of things that are blue:
marbles, matchboxes, paper, string,
    and candy wrappers, too.

"I can't stand red, tho' green's okay,
    but when a nice green berry
turns ripe and red, you can be sure
    I toss it in a hurry!"

God has no favorite colors,
   like the bowerbird's favorite blue.
He loves red and yellow, black and white—
   that means He loves you, too!

Bible Verse:

"He hath made everything beautiful" (Eccles. 3:11, KJV).

Questions:

1. What color does the bowerbird like best?
2. What color do you like best?
3. Why do people have different colored eyes and skin?
4. Does God have a favorite color?

Prayer:

Dear Jesus, You made so many pretty colors. You made different-colored people, too, and You love them all. So do I.

Salmon

Salmon, salmon, where are you going
   on this fine spring day?
"To the great big wide ocean
   to eat and grow and play."

Salmon, salmon, where are you going,
   now that you are four?
"I'm swimming upstream to the place
   where I was born before."

Salmon, salmon, how will you get there?
   The waterfalls are steep.
"I'll try and try and try some more
   o'er each obstacle to leap."

Bible Verse:

"I can do all things through Him who strengthens me"
(Phil. 4:13).

Questions:

1. Why was the salmon going to the ocean?
2. Where did he go when he was four years old?
3. How did he get over the waterfalls?
4. What is a hard thing you must do?
5. Who will help you?

Prayer:

Dear Jesus, the salmon tries and tries again. He doesn't give up. Help me not to give up either. Thank You for helping me do hard things.

Hummingbird

She weighs less than a penny,
    tiny to be sure.
She moves her wings so very fast
    they look just like a blur.

Her nest is like a thimble,
    her eggs the size of peas.
Her babies are so tiny,
    you can't see them in the leaves.

But Mrs. Hummingbird is so brave.
    If enemies come near,
no matter how big and fierce they are,
    she attacks them without fear.

Bible Verse:

"Do not fear, for I am with you" (Isa. 41:10).

Questions:

1. How big is the hummingbird's nest?
2. How big are her eggs?
3. What does she do when enemies come to harm her babies?
4. Who helps you not to be afraid?

Prayer:

Dear Jesus, I don't need to be afraid, because You are with me. Help me always to remember.

Earthworm

An earthworm has no ears or eyes,
    nor has he teeth or nose.
But still he does a job for man
    no matter where he goes.

He crumbles up the dirt so that
    the rain can get way down
to the roots of plants and trees
    all buried in the ground.

Earthworm, you are ugly.
    All will agree 'tis true.
But you are useful in God's plan.
    Hurrah, hurrah, for you!

God also has a plan for me,
    though I am still quite small.
I can help my parents,
    and I can share my ball.

Bible Verse:

"Who has despised the day of small things?" (Zech. 4:10).

Questions:

1. Do you think earthworms are handsome?
2. What kind of work does the earthworm do?
3. How big do you have to be before God can use you?

Prayer:

Dear Jesus, thank You that You can use me even if I am not big and strong. I can help Mommy and Daddy and share my toys.

Snail

Snail, O snail, you are very slow;
   you must be often late!
But you are strong, for you can pull
   two hundred times your weight!

You have something quite unique—
   twenty-five-thousand teeth!
And you repair them all by yourself.
   Now that is quite a feat!

The God who made you made me, too.
   I also am a prize.
I thank You, Lord, for hands and feet,
   for ears, nose, mouth and eyes.

Bible Verse:

"Who does great things . . . and wondrous works without number" (Job 9:10).

Questions:

1. How much can a snail pull?
2. How many teeth does he have?
3. Who is his dentist?
4. How are you special?

Prayer:

Dear Jesus, You made even snails special. Thank You for making me special, too.

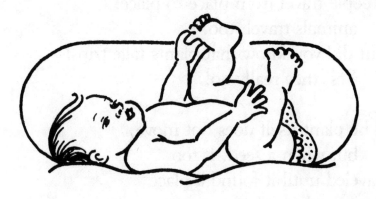

Traveling Plants

People travel from place to place;
    animals travel, too.
But did you know that plants take trips?
    Yes, they really do!

The plant itself does not move,
    but when a seed, it too
traveled until it found a place
    to make a plant so new.

Strawberry plants send out runners;
    they settle close to home.
Other seeds are carried by birds,
    for hundreds of miles they roam.

The seed from a dandelion
   goes floating through the air.
The lotus seed travels by water
   when it goes anywhere.

God has a plan for little seeds;
   He has a plan for you, too.
He wants you to grow up to know Him
   and to please Him in all that you do.

Bible Verse:

"I know the plans that I have for you, declares the Lord"
(Jer. 29:11).

Questions:

1. How do seeds travel?
2. What do the seeds become?
3. What plan does God have for you?

Prayer:

Dear Jesus, help me to grow up to please You in all I do.

Animal Talk

Animals don't talk like we do,
    but they make sounds to express
their wants, their needs, their feelings
    of sadness or happiness.

Sometimes they warn of danger
    other animals of their family.
Sometimes they say, "Get out of here.
    This is *my* place to be."

Bees communicate through a dance,
    chickens cluck, birds call,
dogs bark, wolves howl, frogs splash.
    It's all very wonderful!

But no animal in all the earth
 can do what you can do—
talk to God in prayer and then
 listen as He talks to you.

Bible Verse:

"Then God said, Let the earth bring forth living creatures"
(Gen. 1:24).

Questions:

1. How many animal sounds can you think of?
2. What can you do that animals can't do?

Prayer:

Thank You, Jesus, that You talk to me and I talk to You.

Golden Plover

Golden Plover is a small bird,
    but a champion flier is he.
He flies nonstop over 2,000 miles,
    nonstop over the sea.

For his long trip this small bird
    prepares so carefully—
takes practice flights to get in shape,
    eats food for energy.

The trackless ocean has no signs;
    there is no place to rest.
But the golden plover has no fear;
    he's a champion flier—the best.

Someday we too shall take a trip,
 for which we must prepare,
to go to Heaven when we die
 or meet Jesus in the air.

Bible Verse:

"I will dwell in the house of the Lord forever" (Ps. 23:6).

Questions:

1. How many miles does the golden plover fly nonstop?
2. How does he prepare for his long trip?
3. What long trip will we take someday?
4. How do we prepare for that trip?

Prayer:

Dear Jesus, help me to be ready to meet You someday.

Starfish

Though the starfish lives in the ocean,
  he does not swim at all.
He walks on hundreds of suction feet;
  they help him not to fall.

Those suction feet open up shells
  of oysters and clams for his dinner.
He presses and pulls and doesn't give up
  until he is the winner.

The starfish has no head or tail,
  so backward he never goes.
If he loses a part of his body,
  a new part quickly grows.

Bible Verse:

"Come and see the works of God" (Ps. 66:5).

Questions:

1. How does a starfish move about in the ocean?
2. What kind of feet does he have?
3. What happens when he loses part of his body?
4. Who made such a wonderful creature?

Prayer:

Thank You, Lord, for the wonderful things You have made.

Peacock

The peacock has a gorgeous tail.
    He's the king of birds, you know.
He raises his tail, bows and struts.
    He puts on quite a show.

Baby peacock is not so fine;
    his tail is small and gray.
He has nothing at all to strut about,
    but he struts anyway.

Does baby peacock know that he
    will gorgeous be someday,
the king of birds, a sight to see,
    and so he acts that way?

If you love Jesus and follow Him,
    you'll be a king someday, too!
The peacock's tail does not compare
    with the glory awaiting you!

Bible Verse:

"[He] hath made us kings and priests" (Rev. 1:6, KJV).

Questions:

1. Why does the beautiful peacock strut and bow?
2. Why does the plain baby peacock strut and bow?
3. What are you going to be someday if you love Jesus?

Prayer:

Dear Jesus, thank You that I will reign with You someday.

Animal Homes

There is a place for everything.
The pine-needle covered ground
where leaves, twigs and dead branches lie
is where insects will be found.

The next layer in the woodlot
is small plants with tender stems.
There rabbits, frogs and turtles feed;
what a cozy home for them!

The shrub level is the home of
mammals large and small.
Young trees provide a place for birds;
large trees reign over all.

God has a place for each to live—
 a hole, a log, a tree,
or maybe it's a house and yard,
 a perfect place for me!

Bible Verse:

"God, who richly supplies us with all things to enjoy" (1 Tim. 6:17).

Questions:

1. Where do most insects make their home?
2. Where do the rabbits and frogs live in the woods?
3. Where do the fox and deer stay?
4. Where is your place?

Prayer:

Dear Jesus, thank You for giving the animals and me homes just right for us.

Bees

When Baby Bee leaves her cocoon,
    she has one day to rest,
but after that she must work hard;
    she has to do her best.

Her job may be to feed larvae
    with jelly from glands in her head,
or she may flap her wings to
    ventilate the hive instead.

There are many other jobs to do;
    the hive must have a guard.
Some bees must make combs out of wax
    where honey will be stored.

The bees' most important work
  is gathering nectar sweet
to make into honey for the bees;
  they must have food to eat.

She sips the nectar from the flowers—
  it's sweet as sweet can be.
Not only bees like honey—it's
  a healthful treat for me!

Bible Verse:

"Work with your hands" (1 Thess. 4:11).

Questions:

1. When does Busy Bee start to work?
2. What are some of the jobs bees must do?
3. What are your jobs?

Prayer:

Dear Jesus, help me to do my jobs willingly and carefully.

Bats

Bats sleep all day long
    and venture out at night.
How do they find food in the dark?
    Surely not by sight.

They find their food by listening;
    that's how their prey they track.
They send out sounds and then they hear
    the echoes that come back.

Their ears are used for other things,
    though it's too dark for sight.
Echoes guide them 'round obstacles,
    provide collision-free flight.

You, too, can know the way to go
   if you listen to God's Word.
That is the secret—listen well,
   then obey what you have heard.

Bible Verse:

"He who listens to me shall live securely" (Prov. 1:33).

Questions:

1. How is the bat able to find food in the dark?
2. How does he find his way in the dark?
3. How do we know the right way to go?

Prayer:

Dear Jesus, help me to always listen to what You say to me.

Lions

The lion's related to my cat—
    they both have padded feet.
They both sneak up on their prey
    when they want something to eat.

The lion is the forest king,
    because he's fierce and strong.
Other animals are afraid of him;
    his teeth are sharp and long.

The Bible says there's another kind
    of lion, oh, so strong.
It's Satan who comes to bother us
    and tempt us to do wrong.

I'm glad there is someone stronger
than Satan, my enemy.
It's Jesus who will surely save
a little child like me.

Bible Verse:

"As for me, I shall call upon God, and the Lord will save me" (Ps. 55:16).

Questions:

1. How can lions sneak up on other animals?
2. Why is the lion the king of the forest?
3. What does the Bible call Satan?
4. How can we escape from his temptations?

Prayer:

Dear Jesus, thank You for saving me from Satan's power.

Praying Mantis

When a praying mantis is born,
  she is tiny, tiny, wee.
She hides in grass and looks around
  for insects smaller than she.

As she grows, she eats larger bugs,
  but I am sorry to relate,
the mantis is so greedy,
  she even eats her mate!

The mantis crosses her forelegs,
  she looks like she's in prayer;
but she is just pretending
  to have a saintly air.

Sometimes boys and girls pretend
to be Christians when they're not.
But you can stop pretending—
ask Jesus into your heart.

Bible Verse:

"Believe in the Lord Jesus, and you shall be saved" (Acts 16:31).

Questions:

1. Why is the praying mantis given that name?
2. In what is the mantis most interested?
3. How can we be real, not pretend, Christians?

Prayer:

Dear Jesus, I believe in You and want You in my heart.

Cleanup Committee

God has a special cleanup gang
    to eat animals that die.
The vulture likes that kind of meal—
    we certainly wonder why.

He has a very special beak
    God gave him for his prey,
and powerful wings that help him take
    his dinner far away.

There is another cleanup squad
    that tidies up the ground.
It is the molds that feed upon
    dead things that they have found.

They make the dead leaves disappear,
    the rotting branches, too,
which go right back into the ground,
    make way for something new.

God likes things neat and clean, you see;
    He doesn't like a mess.
What should you do about your room?
    I think that you can guess!

Bible Verse:

"But prove yourselves doers of the word, and not merely hearers" (James 1:22).

Questions:

1. What birds are on God's cleanup committee?
2. What takes care of dead leaves and branches?
3. Who is the cleanup committee for your room?

Prayer:

Dear Jesus, help me to keep my room neat and clean the way You like it.

Dogs

Dogs make wonderful pets—
   they romp and play with you;
they lick your face and chase your balls,
   but that's not all they do.

Some dogs are guards—they bark a lot
   if someone comes to harm.
The barking wakes the master up;
   they sound a sure alarm.

Some dogs find people who are lost
   in mountains, woods or snow.
They even search for criminals;
   they know just where to go.

Some special dogs are trained to help
 blind people find their way.
Do you wonder how they can?
 They learn first to obey.

Obedience—that's the secret;
 nothing else will do.
When we obey our Father,
 He can use us, too!

Bible Verse:

"We will be obedient!" (Ex. 24:7).

Questions:

1. What are some things dogs do for man?
2. How can they learn to do these things?
3. What kind of boys and girls can God use?

Prayer:

Dear Jesus, help me to be obedient to You and to my parents.

Water

What do you think of water,
　　that colorless liquid you drink?
Do you take it for granted
　　as you turn it on in the sink?

There is water in juice and water in milk,
　　water in potatoes and bread,
water in every food you eat;
　　there's water in your blood.

Nothing can live without water—
　　plants, animals, you or I.
Without this precious liquid,
　　everything would die.

Jesus is the Water of Life—
   eternal life He'll give.
"Believe in Me," He says to you;
   "Come to Me and live."

Bible Verse:

"I give eternal life to them" (John 10:28).

Questions:

1. Why is water important?
2. What does Jesus call himself?
3. What does Jesus give those who believe in Him?

Prayer:

Thank You, Jesus, for this wonderful gift of eternal life.

Fireflies

Have you ever seen fireflies
    flit about on a summer night?
They have tiny lights within their tails
    that sparkle, oh, so bright!

Catch a few and put them in a jar.
    You'll be able to read by their light.
If you tie a firefly on your toe,
    it will guide you in the night.

God's Word is a lamp unto our feet,
    a light that shows the way,
not only how to get to Heaven,
    but how to live each day.

Bible Verse:

"Thy word is a lamp to my feet, and a light to my path"
(Ps. 119:105).

Questions:

1. Where does the firefly carry his light?
2. Who gave him this light?
3. Where do we get light to show us the way to Heaven and how to live?

Prayer:

Dear Jesus, thank You for the light of Your book, the Bible.

Shadows

When I go out into the sun,
   my shadow follows me.
Sometimes it's like a giant,
   Sometimes it's tiny wee.

The great big tree in our front yard
   has a shadow, too.
It makes a lovely shady spot
   for me to play with you.

The biggest shadow of them all
   is night, the time to sleep.
The earth hides the sun from our eyes,
   We don't even get a peek.

The valley of the shadow
   is a scary place, they say.
But Jesus says He'll stay with me
   and keep me all the way.

Bible Verse:

Jesus said, "I will never leave thee" (Heb. 13:5, KJV).

Questions:

1. Where does your shadow come from?
2. What is the biggest shadow?
3. Who is with us in "the valley of the shadow"?

Prayer:

Dear Jesus, I am glad You will never leave me alone.

Stars

When you look up into the sky
   on a clear autumn night,
you see hundreds of tiny stars
   that sparkle oh so bright.

They look wee tiny way up there,
   but they are really not.
It's only that they're far away
   so they look like just a dot.

There are so many, many stars,
   we could never count them all.
But God has names for every one;
   they're at His beck and call.

Millions of people live in our world;
    God knows each one of them, too.
He knows your name, think of that!
    He has great plans for you!

Bible Verse:

"How precious also are Thy thoughts to me, O God!" (Ps. 139:17).

Questions:

1. Why do the stars look small?
2. How many stars are there?
3. How many have a name?
4. Does God know your name?

Prayer:

Dear Jesus, I'm glad You know me and are planning great things for me.